The Standard Publishing Company, Cincinnati, Ohio.
A division of Standex International Corporation.
© 1992 by The Standard Publishing Company
All rights reserved.
Printed in the United States of America
99 98 97 96 95 94 93 92   5 4 3 2 1

Library of Congress Cataloging-in-Publication Data
Stortz, Diane M.
Five small loaves and two small fish :
Jesus' feeding of the five thousand / retold by Diane Stortz ;
illustrated by Joe Stites.
ISBN 0-87403-953-3
Library of Congress Catalog Card Number 91-45509

Five Small Loaves
and
Two Small Fish

Jesus' feeding of the five thousand
retold by

Diane Stortz

illustrated by Joe Stites

S
STANDARD
PUBLISHING

On a hill, listening to Jesus, sat a boy.
His stomach was growling.

The boy had forgotten
to eat his lunch.
No one in the crowd
had eaten anything since morning.
Listening to Jesus
was too wonderful
to stop to eat.

But Jesus' disciples were getting worried.
"It's getting late," they said to Jesus.
"Send the people away
so they can go and buy food."

"You can give them
something to eat," said Jesus.

"How can we do that?"
asked the disciples.
"We don't have enough money
to buy food for all these people!"

But Jesus knew what He was going to do.

"How many loaves of bread do you have?" Jesus asked. "Go and see."

One of the disciples, Andrew,
found the hungry boy

and the hungry boy's lunch—

five small loaves

and two small fish.

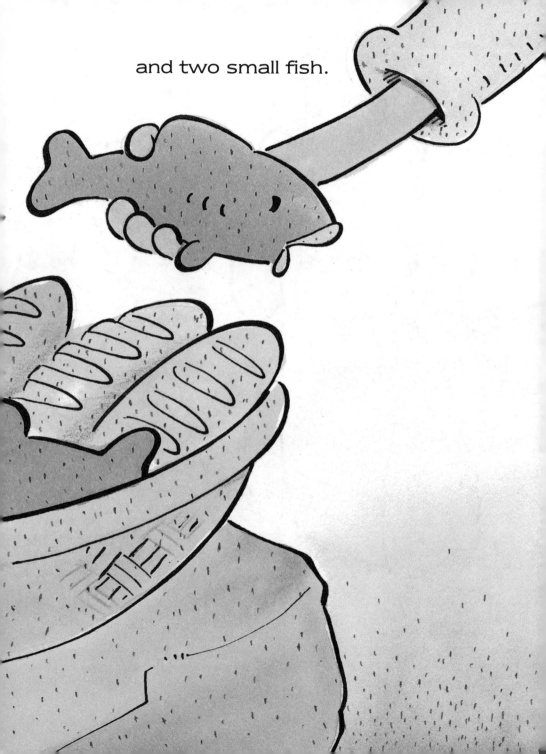

"Please come with me
to see Jesus," said Andrew.
"And bring your lunch!"

Jesus smiled at the hungry boy.
"Tell the people to sit in groups,"
He said to His disciples.

Jesus thanked God for the food.

Then He broke the loaves and fish
into pieces just the right size to eat.

Everyone got some.
Everyone got as *much* as he could eat,

and there was enough left over
to fill twelve baskets!

"Jesus is someone special,
sent from God," the people said.

The boy was sure
that they were right!